# *the* **Guinea** pig

Buying, nutrition, housing, care,
reproduction, health and lots more

# Contents

# Foreword

The book you're holding has been written to give you the basic information you need to be able to keep a Guinea Pig as a pet. It also offers some background information and other things worth knowing. The Guinea Pig is not intended to be a handbook for advanced Guinea Pig-lovers or breeders. The 64 pages in this small book don't have room for that in-depth information.

Besides general information such as origins, history, buying, housing, care, reproduction, health and diseases, we briefly cover small animals as a hobby. A separate chapter is devoted to special Guinea Pigs. These are Guinea Pigs closely related to the tame Guinea Pig we know. Experienced Guinea Pig-lovers and breeders keep them.

The *About Pets* editorial team

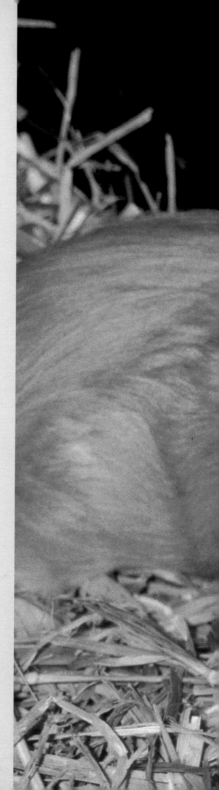

# ibooks

ibooks, inc.
24 West 25th Street
New York, NY 10010

The ibooks World Wide Web Site
Address is:
http://www.ibooks.net

ISBN 0-7434-4527-9
First ibooks, inc. printing
November 2002
10 9 8 7 6 5 4 3 2 1

Senior Consultant Lisa K. Allen, DVM
Cover photograph
copyright © 2002 PhotoDisc, Inc.
Cover design by j. vita

As the purchaser of this book, you are
entitled to access a free electronic book
version of the title for use with
Windows, Macintosh and Palm
computers and PDAs. To access the
"ebook" version, you may log onto
www.ibooks.net, click the "About Pets"
button and follow the directions.

Original title: *de Cavia*

© 1998-2002 Welzo Media Productions bv,

Warffum, the Netherlands

http://www.overdieren.nl

Photos: Dick Hamer,

Rob Doolaard and Rob Dekker

Printed in China

# In general

**The Guinea Pig, also known as the Cavy, is one of the most popular children's pets, but even adults can get a lot of pleasure out of keeping and breeding this little animal. Guinea Pigs are exceptionally friendly animals and are rarely aggressive.**

A Guinea Pig is also ideally sized, not too big (easy for children to handle) and not too small (they can withstand over-enthusiastic children's hands). A Guinea Pig is an animal that doesn't have extreme demands in terms of care or feeding, but you do have to observe a few rules to avoid problems. They need to be fed with care; a poorly-balanced diet can quickly make a Guinea Pig seriously ill.

## Origins

Long before the Spanish conquered South America, Guinea Pigs were kept as pets in Peru and Chile. The Incas bred Guinea Pigs mainly for their meat and fur. The meat (which apparently tastes similar to pork) was regarded as a special delicacy and was eaten at feasts and weddings. These animals probably also played a role in this highly civilized people's religious ceremonies. Mummified Guinea Pigs have been found in Inca tombs.

At the end of the sixteenth century, Spanish explorers and Dutch seafarers brought the Guinea Pig to Europe via Guinea on the West African coast, presumably to provide fresh meat during the long voyage. However, a number of animals escaped the frying pan and arrived in Europe alive. The Guinea Pig was already known of in Europe at the time, because it had been described and illustrated by the Swiss biologist Gessner in 1533.

It was still to be a long time before the Guinea Pig became a popular pet, but Guinea Pigs are known to have been sold by the Dutch to France and England in 1680. At the beginning they were so expensive that only the rich could buy them as a curiosity or as a toy for their children. Particularly in Britain, Guinea Pig lovers tried hard to make the animal better known, but wasn't until after the Second World War that they became really popular.

A side effect was that they were used more and more as experimental animals in laboratories. They played an important role in the fight against tuberculosis and the development of a serum against diphtheria.

## In the wild

Many varieties of Guinea Pig (and other Cavy types) still live in the wild in South America. They belong to the rodent order (*Rodentia*). Rodents form the largest group of mammals; more than half the mammals in the world are rodents. The rodent order comprises more than three hundred families and almost three thousand varieties. In the chart on the next page, you can see what place the Cavy occupies in the mammal hierarchy. The Cavy types that live in the wild differ widely in terms of size and weight. The smallest weigh some three ounces, the largest up to 170 pounds. In length they range from six inches to four feet, but they all have some common characteristics. Their head is relatively large; they all have four toes on their front paws with relatively wide, curved nails. They are all *digitigrades* (walk on their toes) with many similarities in terms of gait. In contrast to other rodents, normal Guinea Pigs cannot climb or stand on their rear paws. They also don't use their forepaws to hold their food. They are not uncommon in their natural habitat, and they have virtually no economic value for man, so they're not hunted on any great scale. The most common variety is the wild Guinea Pig (*Cavia Aperea*). Some experts believe our "tame" Guinea Pig is a descendant of this variety, while others give this honor to the Tschudi Cavia (*Cavia aperea tschudi*). In the chapter *Special Guinea Pigs* you can read more about these wild varieties.

## Name confusion

The tame Cavy is known under many different names. It is often referred to as a Marmot, but the Marmot is not related to the Cavy. It is much larger, has a six-inch tail and belongs to the squirrel family. The word Marmot is probably a dialectic translation from the German name *Meerschweinchen. Meer* means "sea" and *mot* is a medieval word for "pig." In French it is called a *Cochon d'Inde*, meaning "Indies Pig," while in English we know it as the "Guinea Pig." In the United States it is also commonly called a "Cavy."

The largest: Capybara

Although the Guinea Pig and the Degu are related, they cannot be kept in the same cage.

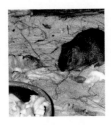

Wild Cavy

## in general

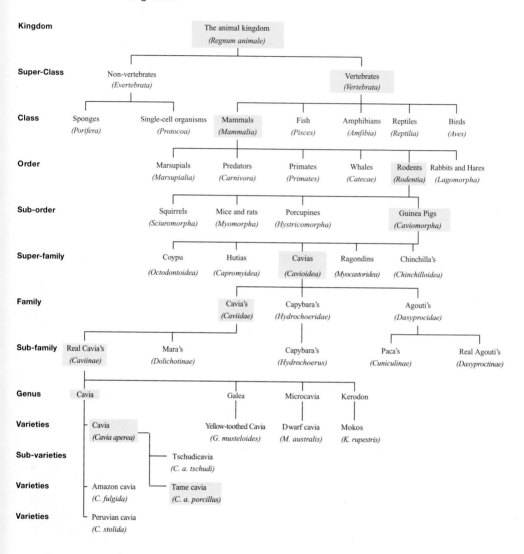

| | | |
|---|---|---|
| **Kingdom** | The animal kingdom *(Regnum animale)* | |
| **Super-Class** | Non-vertebrates *(Everterbrata)* / Vertebrates *(Vertebrata)* | |
| **Class** | Sponges *(Porifera)* · Single-cell organisms *(Protocoa)* · Mammals *(Mammalia)* · Fish *(Pisces)* · Amphibians *(Amfibia)* · Reptiles *(Reptilia)* · Birds *(Aves)* | |
| **Order** | Marsupials *(Marsupialia)* · Predators *(Carnivora)* · Primates *(Primates)* · Whales *(Catecae)* · Rodents *(Rodentia)* · Rabbits and Hares *(Lagomorpha)* | |
| **Sub-order** | Squirrels *(Sciuromorpha)* · Mice and rats *(Myomorpha)* · Porcupines *(Hystricomorpha)* · Guinea Pigs *(Caviomorpha)* | |
| **Super-family** | Coypu *(Octodontoidea)* · Hutias *(Capromyidea)* · Cavias *(Cavioidea)* · Ragondins *(Myocastoridea)* · Chinchilla's *(Chinchilloidea)* | |
| **Family** | Cavia's *(Caviidae)* · Capybara's *(Hydrochoeridae)* · Agouti's *(Dasyprocidae)* | |
| **Sub-family** | Real Cavia's *(Caviinae)* · Mara's *(Dolichotinae)* · Capybara's *(Hydrochoerus)* · Paca's *(Cuniculinae)* · Real Agouti's *(Dasyproctinae)* | |
| **Genus** | Cavia · Galea · Microcavia · Kerodon | |
| **Varieties** | Cavia *(Cavia aperea)* · Yellow-toothed Cavia *(G. musteloides)* · Dwarf cavia *(M. australis)* · Mokos *(K. rupestris)* | |
| **Sub-varieties** | Tschudicavia *(C. a. tschudi)* | |
| **Varieties** | Amazon cavia *(C. fulgida)* · Tame cavia *(C. a. porcillus)* | |
| **Varieties** | Peruvian cavia *(C. stolida)* | |

Satin Cream

# Buying a Guinea Pig

**Buying a pet is a different matter than buying a toy or a pound of sugar. An animal is a living being, and we need to treat it well and responsibly.**

Tri-color longhair

Whether we buy a dog, a cat, a goldfish or a Guinea Pig: all our pets depend on us. If we don't care for them, they become ill, and if we don't give them a proper home they can escape and, sadly, all too often meet their death in the wild. Taking care of one animal may mean (much) more time than another, but in all cases care is something that must happen **every day**.

Whenever you're thinking about buying a pet, get all the information you need **in advance**. Is this the right animal for your family situation? How much care does it need, and do you have the time for it over the long term? What does the animal eat, what kind of cage does it need, does it live alone or is it better to have a

pair or a group? How much will it cost to buy and look after (including veterinarian's bills) and can you afford that? Get the answers to these questions in advance to avoid disappointments and problems later. If you're in any doubt, don't buy the animal!

Before you take your Guinea Pig home, you must be sure you have proper accommodation for it there. After all, you can't keep a rodent in a cardboard box forever.

If you're buying a Guinea Pig for a child, it's important to agree in advance who is going to feed it and keep its home clean. Practice shows that children often promise a lot in their enthusiasm, but don't always keep these promises over time. You must take account of the fact

that a pet needs caring for when you're on vacation or out of the house. The same applies, by the way, when you come home tired after a long day at work or school.

All in all, caring for a pet usually brings lots of pleasure. It's like having a little piece of nature in your home, and Guinea Pigs make excellent pets. They are quiet and calm animals and will almost never bite or scratch, which makes them excellent company for children. Their robustness even makes them suitable for younger children, and they can take rough handling at the hands of a toddler.

## One or more

Guinea Pigs by nature are group or family animals. They feel happier in the company of their counterparts. You can keep a Guinea Pig alone, but then you must give it plenty of attention.

If it doesn't get this attention, it will slowly but surely waste away. A Guinea Pig can also live well together with a small or medium-sized rabbit. However, don't put several adult males together in one home; they won't accept each other.

## Where to buy

Crested

Most Guinea Pigs are sold in pet stores. Pet store owners generally know how to properly look after the animals they sell, but sadly there are some stores that are not so good. You can often spot what kind of store you're dealing with. Are the cages clean? Do all the animals have clean water? Do they look fit and healthy? It is also important that you get complete and honest information about the animal. Most pet stores buy their animals from enthusiasts or serious breeders. These try to breed "perfect" examples, often for shows. If their Guinea Pigs do not meet the strict competition rules, they are selected at a young age to be sold. These animals are usually perfectly healthy, but may not be quite the right color, or they may have a spot of color in the wrong place.

Sadly, there is another type of breeder. These people try to breed as many animals as they can as fast as they can, in an attempt to get rich quick. They pay no attention to the animals' health and don't worry about hygiene or in-breeding. Moreover, many of

the young are separated from their mother when they're still far too young. If you're looking for a good breeder, get in touch with a local small-animal club.

You can also buy a Guinea Pig at one of many animal shows, which are mostly held in the fall and winter. One of these shows is worth a visit even if you're not looking for a Guinea Pig.

Never buy an animal at an open-air market. These are places where "factory-breeders" try to tempt you with their pathetic little animals in tiny cages, almost begging for a better life. Never give in to this temptation. Buying an animal here is keeping this miserable industry going. Profit is these dealers' only motive, and they will only stop when they can no longer make any money.

## Transport

When you buy, or are given, a Guinea Pig, you have to get the animal home. In many cases, this is done in a carton, but this is not the best solution. It would not be the first time (and won't be the last time either) that a Guinea Pig gnaws a hole in such

a box and goes off on a journey of discovery in the shopping bag or the car. So it's better to get a transport container in advance, and you can buy them at any pet store. Make sure it's properly protected, but also ventilated! Never leave the transport container sitting in a car standing in the sun. The high temperature that can result may be fatal for your animal.

## Things to watch out for

If you're planning to buy a Guinea Pig, watch out for the following points:

- The animal must be healthy. A healthy Guinea Pig has clear, bright eyes and is lively. Its genital areas must be clean, and the animal should have no wounds, strange swellings, scale, or crusts. The nose, ears and lips must be clean and dry and not crusted. The coat should be smooth and glossy (except for the shorthaired varieties).
- The Guinea Pig should be well fed, but not fat. It should feel solid and may not display a high back or sunken flanks.
- Watch out for its breathing. Squeaky or rattling breathing may point to an infection. Droppings must be dry and firm; wet, soft droppings can be a sign of an intestinal infection.
- Your Guinea Pig should not be too young or too small. During the first few weeks of its life, the young animal gets antibodies from its mother's milk, which it badly needs. Ask the seller the animal's age. Never buy a Guinea Pig younger than five weeks, or one that seems far too light for its age.
- Nor should your Guinea Pig be too old. Older animals die sooner, of course, but they also find it more difficult to get used to new surroundings. You can recognize older animals by their coat, which is less glossy and may even have bald patches.
- Also check the other animals that share the cage with the one of your choice. Even if the one you want seems healthy, if any of its cage-mates are sick, your new pride and joy may also be carrying an infection.
- Check whether your Guinea Pig is really the same sex as the seller tells you. Many mistakes are still made on this point. Often two "females" suddenly seem to produce young. Adult boars can be recognized by their testicles. On younger animals, an experienced breeder or enthusiast can carefully press the penis out.

# Nutrition and feeding your Guinea Pig

### Pelleted food

Guinea Pigs are herbivores and should receive fresh pelleted Guinea Pig food that can be obtained from a reputable pet store. Guinea Pigs like to eat from clean feeders, so the feeders should be suspended above the bedding. Pelleted food can be supplemented with hay, which promotes growth and helps with digestion.

### Vitamin C

Guinea Pigs, like primates, lack an enzyme which makes vitamin C from dietary sugars, so they must receive extra vitamin C in their diets daily. Vitamin C is added to the pelleted Guinea Pig food, but it does not last on the shelf. The best way to supplement vitamin C is by giving green vegetables daily. Vegetables with the highest vitamin C content include broccoli, kale and parsley.

Lack of extra vitamin C in the diet will result in scurvy. (See section on *Your Guinea Pig's Health*.)

### Water

The idea that Guinea Pigs need only a little to drink is a fable. Even if you give them plenty of green food, they still need fresh water every day. Give them water at room temperature in a drinking bottle. Clean the bottle regularly as poisonous algae can build up inside it. Guinea Pigs sometimes have the habit of drinking from their bottle with a mouth full of food, so it can become dirty or blocked. Check the bottle and replace the water every day.

Hay with herbs

## Snacks and extras

A Guinea Pig is a real rodent. To keep its teeth in good condition it needs something to gnaw on. There are various munchies available in pet stores, but you can also use branches or twigs from willow, fruit, or other deciduous trees. A hard slice of dried bread or some crisp bread are also suitable snacks.

Don't give a Guinea Pig potato chips, cookies, sweets or sugar lumps as extras. These are extremely unhealthy for pets, as they contain too much salt, sugar, and fat. There are enough healthy snacks that you can use to give your Guinea Pig a treat. Of course, not every animal has the same tastes, one Guinea Pig may like something that another won't eat, but parsley, chicory, carrot leaves, rose-hips and kiwis will usually be greeted with pleasure.

Snacks

| Vitamin C in vegetables and fruit (mg per 100 g) | |
|---|---|
| Carrots | 5 mg |
| Endives | 10 mg |
| Apple | 10 mg |
| Tomato | 20 mg |
| Blanched celery | 25 mg |
| Orange | 50 mg |
| Cauliflower | 75 mg |
| Broccoli | 110 mg |
| Chicory | 115 mg |
| Kale | 125 mg |
| Sprouts | 150 mg |
| Paprika | 150 mg |
| Parsley | 170 mg |
| Rose-hip | 500 mg |

Water bottle

# A home for your Guinea Pig

**If you want to keep a Guinea Pig responsibly and give it a comfortable home, it's important to learn about how they live in the wild.**

A Guinea Pig can happily live with a (dwarf) rabbit, but not with other animals!

Even if your Guinea Pig lives in a hutch or a cage at home, it is still possible to design it to be close to their natural living conditions, making the animal feel as comfortable as possible.

## In the wild

The tame Guinea Pig that we keep as pets does not exist in the wild. A possible ancestor, the wild Guinea Pig is found in large numbers in South America. The native population has kept it in semi-captivity for centuries. Even today, countless Guinea Pigs live in and around villages where, close to mankind, they rummage around for food.

The Tschudi Cavia, another candidate as forerunner of our pet Guinea Pig, tends to live closer to nature. It is found mostly in mountainous areas up to as high as 14,000 feet.

Various wild varieties of Cavia live in mountains, on savannas, and in swamps, but tend to avoid the thick tropical rain forests. They live in burrows, in groups of five to ten animals. They prefer to use existing, natural cavities or burrows that other animals have dug. If there's none available, they get to work themselves. Cavia burrow systems are not complex or deep. They only serve as a hideaway and nest.

## Housing in captivity

Guinea Pigs are not overly fussy about their home. They feel more comfortable if they live together with counterparts, but it's not a good idea to keep two boars together if there are also sows nearby. The males will certainly fight if this is the case. A good Guinea Pig home must first be dry and draft-free, but also well ventilated. Drafts and damp are the biggest threats to your Guinea Pigs' health.

As for all pets, the rule "the bigger the better" also applies to your Guinea Pig's home. The minimum size for a single Guinea Pig is 24 x 18 inches. If you keep two or more together, the cage must naturally be bigger.

## Types of cage

The simplest and quickest way to buy a good cage is a visit to the pet store. There you'll find Guinea Pig cages in all shapes and sizes. They mostly consist of a plastic base with a top part of metal wire. Make sure the sides of the base are high enough to prevent your Guinea Pig from throwing hay and sawdust out of the cage.

Indoor cage

An outdoor run is ideal for Guinea Pigs, but must be free from frost.

**A do-it-yourself hutch:**
- Use a hard material for the floor so that urine or water can't soak in (glass, plasticized panels).
- Don't use materials that can splinter if gnawed at.
- Don't use nails or screws in places where they can be gnawed free.
- Don't use plasticized wire netting.
- Don't use wire netting as a floor.
- The cage should get enough light.
- The cage should not stand in the full sun, especially in the summer.
- The cage should be easy to clean.
- Make sure there is good ventilation, but definitely no drafts.
- Humidity must be neither too high, nor too low.

If you're a moderately-skilled do-it-yourself person, you can even make a cage yourself. That way you can build it the way you want, and make it the size you need. In principle, the cage does not need a lid. Guinea Pigs cannot climb or jump so they won't try to escape. But if you have a cat, a dog, a ferret, or some other animal of prey in the house, then you need a lid.

Don't keep a Guinea Pig together with mice, hamsters or rats in the same cage. But Guinea Pigs can get on well together with a rabbit. If you build the cage yourself, put in a second "floor." This should not be higher than six inches and you will need to build a ladder to it. The space under this floor can then serve as a hideaway.

Old aquarium or glass containers are unsuitable for Guinea Pigs because of the lack of ventilation.

## Guinea Pigs indoors
A Guinea Pig can happily live indoors the whole year round; you'll establish good contact, and your animal will be much tamer. A Guinea Pig is a social animal and will frequently announce its presence with its infectious squeaks. If you do keep a Guinea Pig in a (smaller) indoor cage, you must let it run somewhere in the house at least once a day.

## Guinea Pigs outdoors
If you want to let your Guinea Pig enjoy some fresh air, the easiest way is to put it in a cage in the backyard or on the balcony. Only do this in good weather in the spring or summer. Make sure there's plenty of protection from sun and rain. It's important not to take a Guinea Pig directly from a heated room into the cool outside air (or vice versa). Big temperature variations are bad for its health.

You can also keep a Guinea Pig outdoors on a more permanent basis, but you must bring it indoors when the daytime temperature is less than sixty degrees (fall, winter and early spring). A run with a covered section or rabbit hutch is ideal. It must be absolutely frost-free, preferably a double-walled hutch with plenty of hay. In the wild, Cavias also live in mountains and can handle the cold. But after centuries in captivity the tame Guinea Pig has changed so much that it can no longer stand the cold.

Remember that outdoor cages are very attractive to rats, mice and other unwanted guests, but a properly built run of durable materials can keep them out. Rotting parts of an outdoor cage can harbor mold, insects and other pests, so keep it well maintained.

One disadvantage of an outdoor home is that you have a lot less contact with your pet(s). A

Hay

Straw

Pine shavings

Corncob
byproducts

Recycled paper
products

Guinea Pig that lives alone will particularly suffer when kept outdoors. Practice also shows that Guinea Pigs that are kept indoors live substantially longer than "outdoor" Guinea Pigs. Finally, it is not recommended to keep longhaired Guinea Pigs outdoors.

Many different bedding materials are popular for pet rodents. Newer products include aspen shavings, corncob byproducts, and recycled paper products. Pine shavings are most commonly used. They absorb moisture and odors well, and they provide a comfortable bedding material for the animals. Cedar shavings should not be used for Guinea Pigs because of possible liver, skin, and respiratory problems.

### Interior
A cage with only cage litter and nothing else is a very barren home. A Guinea Pig cage must also contain a manger for its hay, which you can buy at a pet store. Water should be given in a drinking bottle that you hang on the outside, with the spout pointing into the cage. There are two small steel balls in the spout and by moving these the Guinea Pig gets water. Any Guinea Pig will quickly get used to a drinking bottle.

Use a heavy, stone dish for dry food. Guinea Pig's like to stand at the dish with their forepaws on the edge. A dish that is too light will then easily tip over. Green food can simply be laid in the cage. Burrow residents by nature, Guinea Pigs like a hideaway. This can be a little wooden hut or box where they can creep into when they need peace and quiet. If their cage is regularly outdoors their hideaway should not have a black or dark-colored roof, otherwise it will get too hot in the sun.

Guinea Pigs are clean animals that will pick their own toilet corner. Clean this corner every couple of days, then you will only need to clean the whole cage out every two weeks or so.

### Dangers
A pet that is reasonably tame and kept in a smallish cage needs to be let out regularly for a run. Sufficient exercise is very important for an animal's health. If you let your Guinea Pig run in the house, backyard or balcony, you need to be aware of some dangers. Watch out for electrical cables. A Guinea Pig will gnaw at anything and they're not equipped to handle 110 volts. Make sure you don't step on your Guinea Pig and that it doesn't get caught in the door (that may sound exaggerated, but it happens!). Watch other pets carefully (dog or cat). Houseplants can be poisonous for a Guinea Pig, so make sure it can't get at them. Don't let it run on a table or high edge; it is a poor judge of

heights and can seriously injure itself in a fall.

Make sure your backyard or balcony is properly fenced off. A Guinea Pig will quickly find any hole, and your neighbor's dog may not be expecting company.

Guinea Pigs are no longer used to bushes and shrubs. They can easily be injured by spikes and thorns. Finally, don't let your Guinea Pig get wet in the rain; in the wind outside, a wet Guinea Pig can get sick in no time at all.

Housing at a breeder

Gold

# Shows

**Many people breed Guinea Pigs as a hobby. They take them to small-animal shows, where they hope to win prizes with their finest examples. The Guinea Pig's appearance, color and coat are subject to strict rules; not everything is permitted.**

Preparation for a show

The perfect Guinea Pig fulfills the standards of the breeders' association.

### The standard

The breeders' association standard describes how Guinea Pigs and other small rodents such as the Rabbit, the Golden Hamster, the Mongolian Gerbil and the tame rat or fancy mouse should ideally look. An animal entered for a competition can earn points in several categories, such as body condition, coat color, and size. Points are deducted for any defects depending on their seriousness. The animal that finally scores the most points is the winner and earns the title "best in show." Guinea Pigs come in many more colorings and markings than those included in the standard.

But a coloring or marking is only officially recognized if it's in the standard. For example: red and gold Guinea Pigs are described in the standard. If a Guinea Pig is entered that is neither red (a warm maroon color) nor gold (a warm orange color) but something in-between, then it doesn't meet the requirements and will get a medium or poor score in the "color" category. If you are interested in breeding and showing Guinea Pigs, you should contact the American Cavy Breeders Association or the American Rabbit Breeders Association for further details on the specifics of the standard for Guinea Pigs. Both organizations hold officially-sanctioned shows for Guinea Pig enthusiasts. (Refer to the *Facts on the Web* section.)

Silver agouti

Blue

Black

# Breeds and colorings

**It would be going too far to describe all the breeds, colorings and markings of the Guinea Pig in this book. After all, that's what the breed standard is for.**

Japanese

But to give you some idea about the colorful and varied world of the Guinea Pig, we will briefly cover a number of breeds, colorings and markings in this chapter.

**Breeds**
There are thirteen recognized breeds of Guinea Pigs, distinguished mainly by their coat structure. Short-coated breeds include: Abyssinian, Satin Abyssinian, American, Satin American, Teddy, Satin Teddy, and White Crested. The long-coated breeds include: Coronet, Peruvian, Satin Peruvian, Silkie, Satin Silkie, and Texel.

The Satin Guinea Pigs are distinguished from their counter-parts by their "satin sheen," caused by the hollow hair shaft.

The Coronet Guinea Pig wears a crest of fur as a "crown" on its forehead. The Peruvian variety has two rosettes on its hind body.

**Colorings and markings**
A coloring is a group of colors that belong together. There are four main groups of colorings and markings: the agoutis, the single-colored types (called "selfs"), the solid group, and the marked group.

Agouti is a speckled coloring, but also a natural coloring that occurs in the wild. The speckling comes about because the hairs have a tip of a different color to the rest (usually black). Guinea Pig enthusiasts refer to this as "ticking" or "wild color pattern." Agouti Guinea Pigs come in

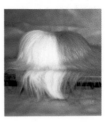

Longhair Brindle

recognized ticking patterns are golden solid, silver solid, and dilute solid.

The marked group includes the varieties with distinctive markings. Broken color Guinea Pigs have a patched appearance made up of two or more recognized colors. Dalmatian Guinea Pigs have a spotted color on a white background. Dutch Guinea Pigs have a blaze, cheek circles, and rear foot stops. The Himalayan variety has a white body color with black points on the feet, nose, and ears. The Tortoise Shell Guinea Pig has red and black-patched markings, while the Tortoise Shell and White variety has red, black, and white-patched markings.

three varieties. Golden Agouti Guinea Pigs have red hair tips with black base color. Silver Agoutis have white tips on a black base. All other base/tip combinations are known as Dilute Agouti.

The self-colorings are of only one color. The following colors are recognized: black, chocolate (dark brown), lilac (bluish with a reddish glow), beige (dark cream color with a gray shimmer), red (warm chestnut red), red-eyed orange (warm orange), cream (light cream color) and white. A white Guinea Pig may have red or dark (brown or blue) eyes.

Solid refers to both a ticking pattern and a color grouping. The recognized solid colors/patterns are brindle (intermixing of red and black hairs), roan (intermixing of a solid or agouti color with white), dilute solid, golden solid, or silver solid. Solid is also a ticked color pattern similar to agouti. The

# Special Guinea Pigs

**Apart from the tame Guinea Pigs we know so well, there are a number of other Cavy varieties, some of which are closely related to "our" Guinea Pig and others somewhat less closely related.**

Rock Cavy

### The wild Cavy

Because no one knows exactly from which variety the tame Guinea Pig descended, we can't say for sure that this is its wild form. In terms of build, the Wild Cavy (*Cavia aperea*) certainly seems like the twin of the tame Guinea Pig. It sports a pretty, red-brown fur with black ticking and is less plump than the tame Guinea Pig.

Special Cavia varieties have been kept in some zoos (including Berlin Zoo) for some time. Breeding of the wild Cavy has met with mixed success, so the population is not that big. One assumes that care and reproduction of the wild Cavy is identical to that of its tame counterpart.

### The Weasel Guinea Pig

The Weasel Guinea Pig, or Cui, (*Galea musteloides*) is not so closely related to the tame Guinea Pig and belongs to another genus (*Galea*). The Weasel Guinea Pig is an animal that lives in groups and is active during the day.

Young are born the whole year round. After a pregnancy of 54 days, the mother gives birth to a litter of one to seven babies. They weigh approximately four ounces at birth and are suckled for 23 days.

There are a few Weasel Guinea Pigs kept in captivity. Some years ago they were bred fairly successfully, but for some unknown reason this has stagnated. The

Weasel Guinea Pig is more slender than the real Guinea Pig. Its coat is a speckled gray in color.

## The Rock Cavy

The Rock Cavy (*Kerodon rupestris*) is also known as the "Mountain Cavy" and, in contrast to other Cavy varieties, it is an excellent climber and jumper. In the wild, Rock Cavies live in trees and along rocky slopes. They move along balancing on thin branches. At certain times, the Rock Cavy is also active at night. Females give birth to their young once or twice a year. Just like the other Cavy varieties, Rock Cavies don't require elaborate care.

## The Tschudi Cavy

The Tschudi Cavy (*Cavia aperea tschudi*) is a sub-variety of the wild Cavy. Some experts regard this sub-variety as the ancestor of the tame Guinea Pig. In the wild, it lives on the slopes of the Andes mountains (central Chile), where it is found at heights up to 14,000 feet. This variety of Cavy lives mainly on grasses and herbs.

Apart from the varieties we've described above, we also know of the Dwarf Cavy (*Microcavia australis*), the Amazon Cavy (*Cavia fulgida*) and the Peruvian Cavy (*Cavia stolida*). However, these varieties are quite rare and little is known about them. They are also not kept in captivity.

The wild Guinea Pig is common in South America.

Weasel Guinea Pig

nutria

hutia

mara

A number of distant relatives of the Guinea Pig.

chinchilla

# Reproduction

**If you let a male and female Guinea Pig live together, there's a very good chance you'll get additions to the family. You need to be sure in advance whether you really want to start breeding Guinea Pigs.**

A litter of baby Guinea Pigs is nice, but after the second or third, it can become difficult to find good homes for the young. So think about reproduction (wanted or not) when you buy the animals. If you want a male and a female, but no young, you can keep them in separate cages. A male can also be castrated.

Guinea Pigs don't bear young as often as mice or hamsters. Without some form of birth control, a pair will produce a litter of two to five young a maximum of four times a year.

### Male or female
It is normally not a simple matter to tell the difference between the sexes. You have to examine them closely under the tail. Like with most rodents, you can tell the difference by the distance between the anus and the genital opening. This distance is much larger on males than on females. On full-grown males you can also see the shape of the scrotum.

### In-breeding
A responsible breeder will never mate any male with any female, because of the risk of in-breeding. For example, if you've got a brother and sister from neighbors, it's best not to breed with them. If these animals produce young, this is a serious form of in-breeding, and who can guarantee that the neighbor's litter wasn't also produced by a brother and sister?

One occasion of in-breeding is certainly not a disaster, but several times in succession will quickly show the results. The young get smaller and weaker with each litter, less young are born and congenital abnormalities can also appear.

## Mating

Wait until your Guinea Pigs are two to three months old before breeding. At this age, the female's bones are still supple enough that they can stretch during the birth. Females that first give birth at an older age have much more difficulty during the birth.

Guinea Pigs don't like mating in the open. They are very discreet and mate when nobody can see. Only one mating session can take place when the sow is in season (ready to mate). Her season is accompanied by a lot of agitation within the Guinea Pig community. A sow goes into season once every 16 days for a period of a few hours. A membrane in the vagina breaks during her season, allowing mating to take place. The boar leaves a wax-like plug in the vagina to prevent sperm flowing out.

A pregnant Guinea Pig will become very round.

## Pregnancy and birth

Pregnant Guinea Pigs can become very fat, although sometimes you may notice nothing at all until three-quarters of the pregnancy has passed. The Guinea Pig's pregnancy lasts some 59–72 days. Guinea Pigs are sensitive to stress, so give the mother-to-be plenty of peace and quiet. Towards the end of the pregnancy, the female is often so heavy that she can barely waddle her way around the hutch. Her body weight may increase by between 50–75 percent.

The birth can usually take place in the cage. In principle, the male can be present, but the sow is ready to mate again within 24 hours after the birth, so it is advisable to house the male somewhere else at this time. The birth usually goes smoothly and quickly. All the young are born within 15–30 minutes.

When a baby is born, the mother licks open the embryo sac and bites through the umbilical cord. Never touch the young with your bare hands as the mother will reject them because of the smell.

## Development

The reason for such a long pregnancy is that young Guinea Pigs are born fully developed and fully covered in fur with eyes and ears open. They can even run straight after being born. Young animals born in this way are called *precocial*. Because Guinea Pigs can flee from predators immediately after birth, their parents never build a real nest or burrow. The young animals' stomachs are fully developed and ready for solid food, but they do take their mother's milk for about a month.

# Your Guinea Pig's health

**Fortunately, Guinea Pigs generally have few health problems. A healthy example has bright eyes and is lively. Its coat is smooth, soft and regular (except for the short-haired variety). Its rear body is dry and clean.**

A sick Guinea Pig sits withdrawn all the time. Its coat is dull and stands open, as if wet. A sick Guinea Pig is usually listless and curls up quietly in a corner.

## Prevention

The rule that "an ounce of prevention is better than a pound of cure" also applies to small animals such as the Guinea Pig. It's not always easy to cure a sick Guinea Pig. Even a slight cold can prove fatal for a Guinea Pig and the biggest risks to its health are drafts and dampness. There are a few general rules that you can follow if your Guinea Pig is ill:

- If the animal lives together with others in the same cage, remove it as quickly as possible. It may be infectious with the risk to your other animals.
- Keep your animal is a quiet semi-dark place. Stress, crowding and noise won't help it get better.
- Keep your animal warm, but make sure its surroundings are not too hot. The best temperature is 65–70 degrees Farhenheit.
- Don't wait too long before visiting a veterinarian. Guinea Pigs that get sick have little will to live and sometimes die within a few days.
- The patient should always have fresh water, and remember that your animal may be too weak to reach its water bottle.
- Sick animals often eat little or nothing. Give it a small piece of apple or other fruit.

## Digestive system conditions
### Antibiotic-associated enterotoxemia

Certain antibiotics can cause a Guinea Pig to stop eating, have severe diarrhea, and become dehydrated. If antibiotic therapy is necessary, your veterinarian will know the appropriate antibiotics for Guinea Pigs.

### Diarrhea

Several bacterial, parasitic, and viral causes of diarrhea are found in the Guinea Pig. Consulet your veterinarian if diarrhea occurs.

### Malocclusion

Guinea Pigs' teeth grow continually, and if the teeth are not lined up correctly, the teeth can overgrow causing difficulty eating. Your veterinarian should check the teeth periodically and trim them if needed.

## Respiratory system conditions
### Pneumonia

Bacterial infection can cause pneumonia in Guinea Pigs, causing decreased appetite, discharge from nose and eyes, and difficulty breathing. Treatment by a veterinarian is imperative.

## Skin conditions
### Fungal disease

Guinea Pigs are susceptible to ringworm. Often, caretakers have lesions before the animals show signs of illness. Signs of ringworm include itchy areas of

| Deficiency of | Symptoms | Found in |
|---|---|---|
| Protein | Poor coat, hair loss, pneumonia, infertility and poor growth of young animals, aggression (both with too much and too little) | Peas, beans, soy, cheese |
| Vitamin A | Pneumonia, damage to mucous membrane or eyes, growth problems, diarrhea and general infections, cramps, small litters | Root vegetables, egg yolk, fresh greens, bananas and other fruit, cheese |
| Vitamin B complex | Hair loss, reduced fertility, weight loss, trembling, nervous symptoms, anemia, infections | Oat flakes, greens, fruit, clover, dog biscuits, grains |
| Vitamin C | The Guinea Pig produces this itself, deficiency rarely a problem | Greens, fruit |
| Vitamin D | Growth problems, poor bone condition. Too much vitamin D causes calcium loss in bones and calcium deposits in blood vessels | Dairy products, egg-yolk |
| Vitamin E | Infertility, muscle infections, nervous problems, bleeding and poor growth of young animals | Egg yolk, sprouting grains, fresh grains, greens |
| Vitamin K | (Nose) bleeding, poor healing of wounds and growth problems. Normally produced in the animal's intestines. | Greens |
| Calcium | Lameness, calcium loss in bones and broken teeth | Mineral preparations, dairy products, varied diet |
| Potassium | Weight loss, heart problems and ascitis, wetness in open abdominal cavity | Fruit |
| Sodium | Can only occur with serious diarrhea | Cheese, varied diet |
| Magnesium | Restlessness, irritability, cramps, diarrhea and hair loss | Greens, grains |
| Iron | Anemia, stomach and intestinal disorders, infertility | Greens, grains, meat |
| Iodine | Metabolic disorders and thyroid gland abnormalities | Greens, grains, water |

Round worm

Tape worm

hair loss with crusts. A veterinarian can prescribe the appropriate treatment.

### Parasites
Mites and fleas can infect Guinea Pigs, causing itching and skin lesions. Again, consult your veterinarian for help with the diagnosis and treatment.

### Abscesses
Abscesses can be secondary to bite wounds and are bacterial infections under the skin. A veterinarian will drain the abscess and prescribe appropriate treatment.

### Scurvy
Guinea Pigs cannot make their own vitamin C, so they must receive vitamin C from their food daily. A lack of vitamin C causes scurvy, manifested as loose teeth, rough hair coat, decreased appetite, prolonged wound healing, pain and increased susceptibility to bacterial infections. Treatment with vitamin C is usually effective.

### Malnutrition
The importance of sufficient vitamin C has been mentioned several times in this book. A shortage of vitamin C is the most common deficiency ailment suffered by Guinea Pigs. However, other deficiencies can also lead to disease. The table on page 50 gives an overview of the diseases that can be caused by certain deficiencies.

### Old age
Obviously we hope that your pet will grow old without disease and pain. However, Guinea Pigs live nowhere near as long as humans, and you must reckon with the fact that after just a few years you have an old Guinea Pig to care for. Such an old Guinea Pig will slowly become quieter and get gray hair in its coat, and now it needs a different kind of care. The time for wild games is over; it won't like them any more. Leave your Guinea Pig in peace.

In the last few weeks and days of its life, you will notice its fur decaying and the animal will get thinner. Don't try to force it to eat if it doesn't want to; the end is usually not long off. Guinea Pigs, on average, live about five years. A seven-year old Guinea Pig is very old, but in exceptional cases they can reach the age of eight.

Russian

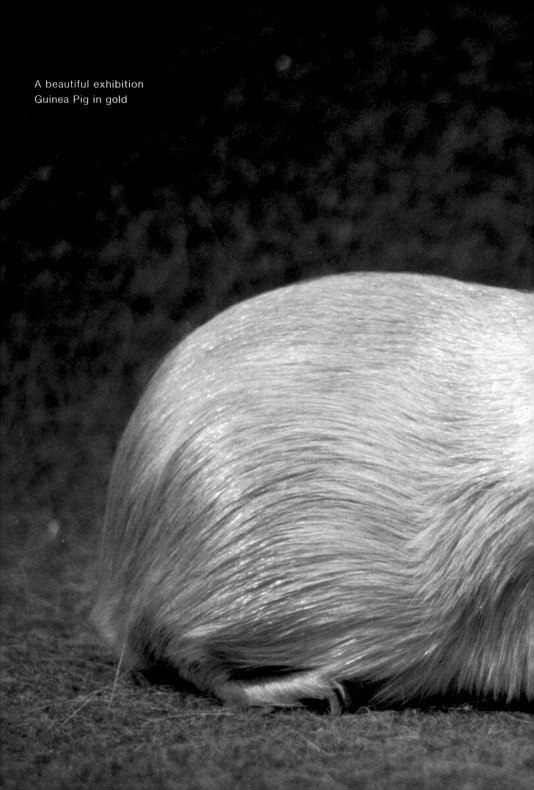

A beautiful exhibition
Guinea Pig in gold

# Tips and facts

- Guinea Pigs and small rabbits can easily be kept together.

- Buy your Guinea Pig at a good pet store, or from a good breeder.

- A Guinea Pig is NOT a Marmot.

- Vitamin C is vital for a Guinea Pig's health. It needs it every day.

- Never leave an animal in a car standing in the full sun.

- Children will be children. Don't let them play with an animal unsupervised.

- Drafts are a Guinea Pig's biggest enemy.

- Don't buy a Guinea Pig too young, but not too old either.

- Visit a small-animal show. It's worth the effort.

- Think before you act. Buying an animal needs careful thought.

- Hay is an important food for Guinea Pigs. You can give it unlimited quantities.

- Guinea Pigs must always be kept free from frost.

- If a Guinea Pig is eating poorly and dribbling, check its teeth.

- Guinea Pigs are pack animals and need company.

- Guinea Pigs mate very discreetly. Be prepared for surprise pregnancies.

- Prevent large variations in temperature.

# Facts on the web

### American Cavy Breeders Association
**www.acbaonline.com**
An organization that promotes the breeding and improvement of the Cavy and secures publicity for and interest in the Cavy as an exhibition, pet, and research animal.

### American Rabbit Breeders Association, Inc.
**www.arba.net**
An organization dedicated to the promotion, development and improvement of the domestic rabbit and Cavy. ARBA encourages each aspect of the rabbit and Cavy industry: fancy (for exhibition), as a pet, or for commercial value.

### Seagull's Guinea Pig Compendium
**www.aracnet.com/~seagull/Guineas/**
One of the most comprehensive sources of Guinea Pig information on the Internet.

### The Guinea Pigs'
### Daily Digest
**www.gpdd.org**
A daily electronic newsletter by and for the Internet Guinea Pigs' fanciers community.

### Rainbow Bridge Tribute
**www.geocities.com/**
A touching site devoted to owners whose Guinea Pigs have died.

### Pet Supplies Guide
**www.petsuppliesguide.com/guineapigs.html**
A site that provides tips on where to find the best deals on pet supplies and pet care.

## The Guinea Pigs' Daily Digest
**www.gpdd.org**
A daily electronic newsletter by and for the Internet Guinea Pigs' fanciers community.

## Cavy Care Site
**www.geocities.com/Heartland/Plains/2517**
This is a gateway to many useful sites about Cavys.

## Dr. Barb Deeb's Guide to Guinea Pig Care
**www.halcyon.com/integra/drdeeb.html**
A site that includes all aspects of basic Guinea Pig care—a good site for new owners or someone wanting to brush up on his or her knowledge about Guinea Pigs.

## Guinea Pigs World
**www.pimms-pages.co.uk**
A fascinating site filled with useful information and tips on "learning the language" of the Guinea Pig and teaching it games.

## Guinea Pigs
**www.guinea-pigs-guinea-pigs.com/links.htm**
The history of the Guinea Pigs and a link to sites including such subjects as entertainment, vet tips, faqs, message boards, discussioin groups, and more.

## OinkerNet Guinea Pigs Worldwide
**www.Oinkernet.com/gplinks.htm**
A site designed to link Guinea Pig breeders and owners around the world.

## Cavyinfo.com International
**www.cavyinfo.com**
An information resource site for Guinea Pig owners. It has a special section on emergency care information.

# Profile of the Guinea Pig

| | |
|---|---|
| Name: | Guinea Pig or Cavy |
| Latin name: | Cavia aperea porcellus |
| Origin: | Wide areas of South America |
| Male: | Boar |
| Female: | Sow |
| Body length: | 9 - 12 inches |
| Weight: | Boar: 28 - 42 ounces |
| | Sow: 26 - 36 ounces |
| Number of teats: | 2 |
| Heart rate: | 230 - 370/minute |
| Breathing rate: | 100 - 150/minute |
| Body temperature: | 99.5 - 103.0 degrees F |
| Sexual maturity: | Boar: 3 months |
| | Sow: 5 months |
| Season cycle: | 16 days |
| Length of season: | 20 - 24 hours |
| Gestation: | 65 - 70 days |
| Number of young: | 2 - 5 |
| Weight at birth: | 1.8 - 5 ounces |
| Suckling period: | 4 weeks |
| Life expectancy: | Average 5 - 7 years (max. 8) |